GOODNIGHT SCRANTON

A Parody

Written and illustrated by Mark Cloud

CHACHABACHA
BOOKS

For Goldie.

Note to the reader:

Don't ever, for any reason, stop reading books, for any reason, ever, no matter what, no matter where, or who, or who you are with, or where you are going, or where you've been, ever, for any reason whatsoever.

In the great green room in Scranton, PA
There was a teapot
And a device for music to play
And a picture of -

The clown playing a tune

And there were words of inspiration

And a CD, and a list, and a golden ticket

And a set of drums when co-workers kick it

Goodnight room

Goodnight regional manager

Goodnight Justice Beaver jumping over the moon

Goodnight Princess Lady

Goodnight Scott's Tots

Goodnight comfy sweater from Pratt
And goodnight box of beets

Goodnight beet farm

And goodnight Jello

Goodnight funky lamp
And goodnight Lake Wallenpaupak

Goodnight blank page

Goodnight chili

And goodnight to the goose
Being so silly

Goodnight www.creedthoughts.gov.www/creedthoughts
And goodnight local rap duo

Goodnight Scranton

Goodnight outer space

Goodnight office workers all over the place

Printed in Great Britain
by Amazon